Two California sea lions lie in the sun off the coast of Mexico. These sleek sea animals come ashore to rest and to raise their young.

Erwin and Peggy Bauer

Amazing Animals of the Sea

Marine Mammals

BOOKS FOR WORLD EXPLORERS
NATIONAL GEOGRAPHIC SOCIETY

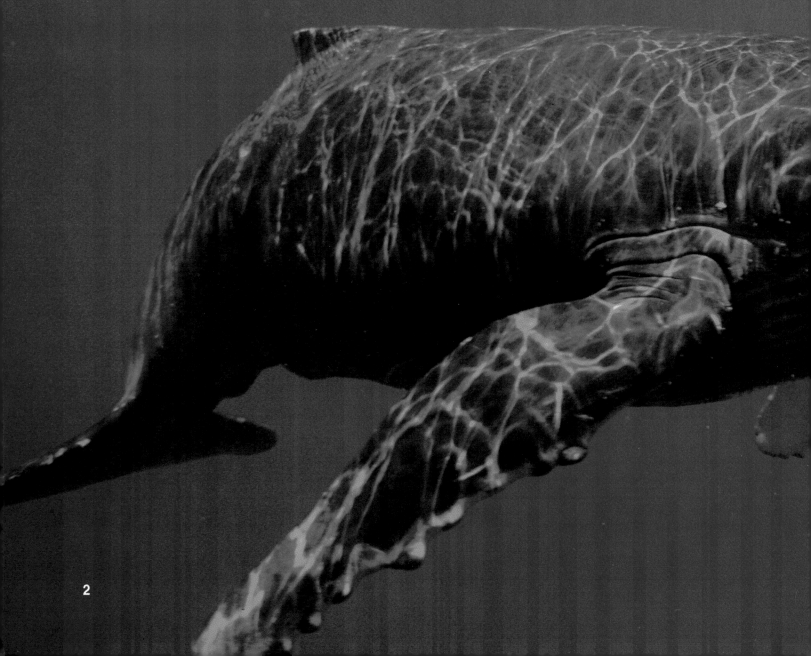

Contents

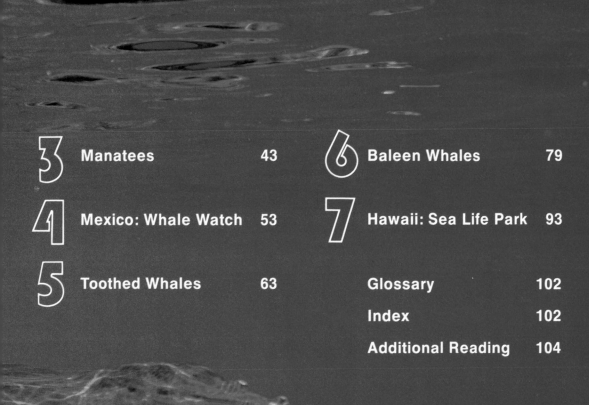

Swimming underwater, a huge humpback whale pushes its body forward with powerful tail fins called flukes. It uses its front flippers to steer.

Graeme Ellis, Nanaimo, B.C.

Cover: Harp seal in Canadian waters surfaces through a hole in the ice to breathe. A thick layer of fat helps protect it from the cold.

Fred Bruemmer

Copyright © 1981 National Geographic Society
Library of Congress ⒸⓅ data: p. 104

What is a marine mammal?

Marine mammals are air-breathing animals that live in the sea. They include whales, dolphins, seals, sea lions, walruses, sea otters, and manatees. These animals depend on the sea for food. They spend most, or all, of their lives in the sea. In fact, "of the sea" is what the word "marine" means.

Mammals that live in the sea have certain things in common with mammals that live on land. They are warm-blooded. They have lungs and breathe air. At some time in their lives, their bodies have some kind of hair. They give birth to live young. And they nurse their young with milk.

Scientists believe the ancestors of all marine mammals once lived on land. Over millions of years, the animals gradually changed. Their bodies became adapted to life in the sea.

Marine mammals vary in size, in appearance, and in the ways they live. Some live in water all the time and could not survive on land. Others spend much time in the sea, but go ashore for certain activities.

Whales and dolphins stay in the sea all their lives. They have smooth, streamlined shapes and look like huge fish or living submarines when they swim. Their front legs have taken the form of flippers. All that remains of the hind legs is a single bone toward the back of the body.

Seals, sea lions, and walruses live both on land and in the sea. They are called pinnipeds. They go ashore to rest and to raise their young. All have four flippers. Flippers help pinnipeds move on land and, of course, swim in the sea.

Whales, dolphins, and the pinnipeds have layers of fat called blubber. The blubber provides warmth and serves as stored food.

The sea otter has no blubber. It relies on a thick,

Newborn harp seal on the ice near Newfoundland drinks warm, rich milk. Born on ice, the baby has white fur that helps hide it from enemies. In two weeks, its birth weight of about 10 pounds (5 kg)* triples. Soon after, it will enter the sea to find its own food.

Fred Bruemmer

*Metric figures in this book are given in rounded numbers.

Clouds of mist shoot into the sky as killer whales surface to breathe (above). The mist is a vapor formed by a mixture of water droplets and air. Whales breathe through nostrils called blowholes on the tops of their heads. When they surface, they blow all the air from their lungs before taking another breath. A fin whale (right) blows a cone-shaped spout of misty air through its two blowholes.

velvety coat to keep it warm. It stays in the sea most of the time. Its hind feet are webbed, like a duck's.

Manatees are perhaps the most unusual of all marine mammals. They live in warm coastal waters, both salty and fresh. They never go ashore. They eat only water plants.

For centuries, people have hunted sea mammals for blubber, meat, hides, fur, and ivory. Some species were nearly wiped out.

In 1972, the United States government passed the Marine Mammal Protection Act. It states that those mammals that are, or may be, in danger of extinction as a result of man's activities should not be permitted to be further reduced in numbers.

Canada, Mexico, and many other countries also have passed laws to protect sea mammals. Some species, with human help, now are steadily increasing in numbers in their ocean homes.

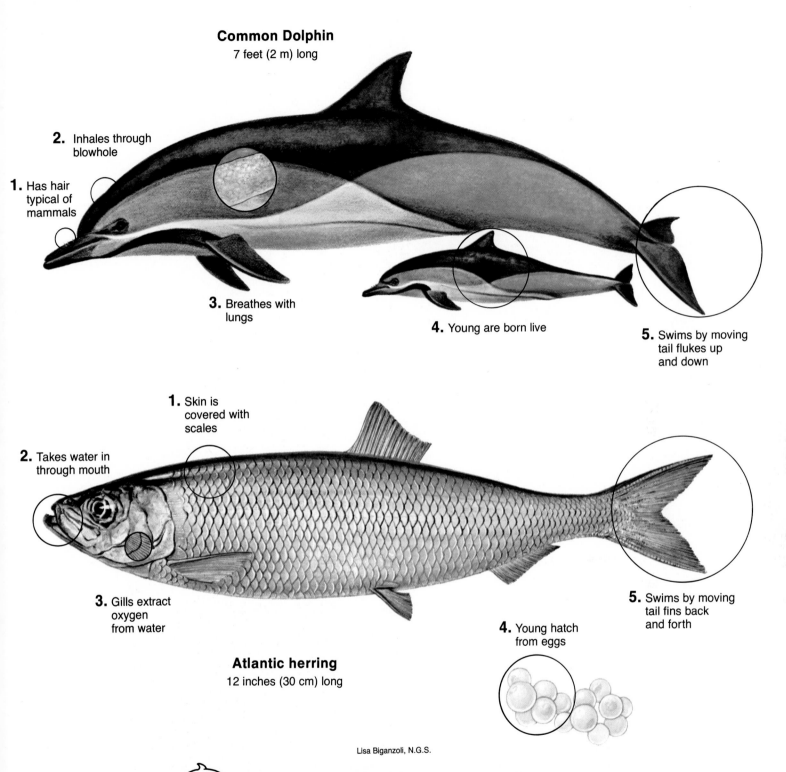

Common Dolphin
7 feet (2 m) long

2. Inhales through blowhole

1. Has hair typical of mammals

3. Breathes with lungs

4. Young are born live

5. Swims by moving tail flukes up and down

1. Skin is covered with scales

2. Takes water in through mouth

3. Gills extract oxygen from water

Atlantic herring
12 inches (30 cm) long

4. Young hatch from eggs

5. Swims by moving tail fins back and forth

Lisa Biganzoli, N.G.S.

Sea mammals and fish inhabit the same watery world. At a quick glance, they look somewhat the same. Both have torpedo shapes. Both have fins and tails. But there are many differences. These drawings of a common dolphin (top) and of an Atlantic herring point out some of the differences between the two creatures.

Pinnipeds

Female Australian sea lion and her pup cross a sandy beach. The mother is at home both on shore and in the sea—like all adult pinnipeds. Sea lion pups are born on shore and do not swim at birth. They spend short periods of time in the water while still young. As they grow, they develop a layer of blubber, or fat, under the skin. Then, with the blubber keeping them warm, they take longer and longer swims.

Suited to life on sea and shore

Millions of seals, sea lions, and walruses live along rocky coastlines, on chunks of floating ice, or on sandy beaches in much of the world. As a group, these animals are called pinnipeds.

Pinnipeds are warm-blooded, air-breathing animals. They spend part of their lives in the water, and part on shore or on floating ice. Some pinnipeds go ashore to mate, and all go there to bear and to raise their young. They return to the sea to feed on fish and other sea animals. Some pinnipeds stay in the water for months at a time.

Pinniped bodies are well suited to life in the sea. A layer of blubber just under the skin provides energy and helps keep the animals warm in icy waters. Torpedo-shaped bodies help pinnipeds swim easily through the water. And the animals can close their nostrils tightly to keep water out. A clear protective layer covers their open eyes as they swim. Pinnipeds see well both underwater and on land. Underwater, their pupils open wide to let in as much light as possible. On land, their pupils close down to small slits.

In the water, pinnipeds swim and steer with their flippers, using them somewhat the way fish use fins. On land, pinnipeds use their flippers as feet. In fact, the word "pinniped" means "fin-footed."

Not all pinnipeds use their flippers in the same way on land. Seals, for instance, are divided into two groups: eared seals and earless seals. Eared seals actually take steps with all four flippers. They bring their hind flippers forward, lifting their bodies off the ground as they move along. Fur seals and sea lions belong in this group. They have ear flaps that stick out from their heads.

Earless seals include all the other seals. They can't

Swimming underwater, a sea lion shows its streamlined shape and delicate pointed ears (below). Because of their ear flaps, sea lions belong to the pinniped group called eared seals. Sea lions have excellent hearing. Scientists think that a sea lion mother can recognize her own baby's call, even among hundreds of crying pups!

David Doubilet

William R. Fraser

Can you spot the ear of this Weddell seal (above)? It's the small, round hole on the side of its head. Because these seals have no outside ear flaps, they belong to a group called earless seals. But they do have ears inside their skulls and can hear well. When seals dive, whether eared or "earless," they close their ear openings tightly to keep water out.

Dotte Larsen

Strong front flippers support the upper body of an antarctic fur seal (left). Webbed hind flippers turn forward when the seal walks on all fours. All eared seals walk this way. But earless seals, such as the Hawaiian monk seal (below), cannot turn their hind flippers forward to walk. They move by humping along on their stomachs.

Lewis Trusty

Scientists believe that the eared seal (left) developed from a land animal resembling a bear (below, left). For almost every bone the bear has, the eared seal has a similar one. But there are differences in size because the seal's bones support its body differently. The shoulder and front leg bones of the seal are much thicker. They support most of the animal's weight on land. Also, the seal's swimming power comes from the front limbs. All leg bones are shorter and enclosed within the body, making for better swimming ability. If you were a seal, your arms and legs would be enclosed, leaving only your hands and feet sticking out. You couldn't move on land as well as you do, but you'd swim better.

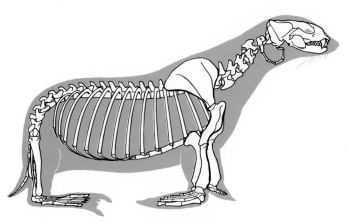
EARED SEAL

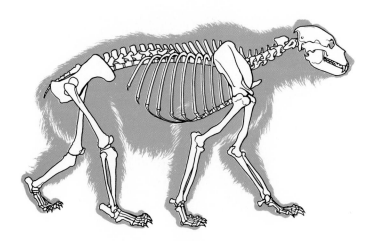
BEAR

turn their hind flippers forward to lift their bodies off the ground. Instead, they move along on their bellies. They look like huge, heaving slugs! Though awkward looking, some can go 15 miles (24 km) an hour on land.

Walruses, enormous as they are, also move faster than you would think. Like the eared seals, they take steps with their front and hind flippers.

To hunt food, all pinnipeds go to sea. Their webbed flippers help them swim swiftly as they chase prey. Excellent divers, they stay underwater for amazingly long periods. A seal that lives in

Lisa Biganzoli, N.G.S.

Sea lions swim underwater off the south coast of Australia. These pinnipeds use their large, winglike front flippers for swimming. They somersault and make graceful turns as they move along. With their large eyes they see well underwater.

antarctic waters holds its breath as long as an hour.

Whiskers on pinniped faces act as feelers to help the animals find prey as it swims by. Walruses also use their hundreds of bristly whiskers to feel for clams buried in the muddy sea bottom.

Mating season is a noisy time for eared seals and elephant seals. Thousands of each kind crowd onto stretches of shoreline where they establish rookeries, or breeding places. Males battle for the best positions in the rookery. Newborn and nursing pups add to the racket.

Most earless seals mate in the water and do not form rookeries. Groups of females gather on land or on ice and give birth. At first, all pinniped pups live on their mothers' rich milk. They gain weight rapidly, forming a layer of blubber to nourish them until they become skilled hunters on their own. They shed their birth coat and grow a new one more suitable to life in the water. Most pinniped pups take care of themselves after a few months. Only the walrus calf stays with its mother for as long as two years. Walrus calves need time to learn to dive and to feed on the ocean floor.

With human coaching, pinnipeds can learn to perform tricks. California sea lions perform at many marine shows, balancing balls on their noses or jumping through hoops. Humans also train pinnipeds to take part in underwater research projects.

Pinnipeds have few natural enemies. Sharks, polar bears, and killer whales hunt them. The greatest threat comes from human beings who kill them for their fur, hides, meat, and ivory. Man has nearly wiped out some species. In recent years, the United States and other nations have passed laws to protect all species of pinnipeds. Many of the animals are making strong comebacks in areas where they had nearly become extinct.

Read more about the different kinds of pinnipeds on the next pages.

Dueling walruses cross tusks during a fight (below). Males often challenge each other this way. Walruses have thick skins and very strong skulls, so such fights rarely result in serious injury to either fighter.

Thick skin, long tusks

On a diet of clams and snails, walruses grow to be huge, thick-skinned animals. There are Atlantic walruses and Pacific walruses. The ones that live in the Pacific Ocean are larger. Almost one-third of an adult walrus is blubber. The blubber protects the animal from the cold and acts as a food source. An adult male weighs about 3,000 pounds (1,361 kg) and grows to be 12 feet (4 m) long.

When a walrus dives, its blood leaves its skin and moves to the organs deep inside the body. This helps keep the animal warm. When the animal surfaces again, it looks pinkish brown. Sunbathing on a rock or on a piece of ice causes the blood to return to the skin. Then the walrus's skin looks its usual reddish brown again.

Walruses live in herds of a hundred or more. They spend most of their time in the water. They mate in the water and swim to floating ice when they give birth. Male walruses, using their long tusks, battle for position in the herd. Most males show scars from the fighting, but serious injuries are few. Tusks don't usually do much damage to hides that are 2 inches (5 cm) thick!

Closely related to the eared seals, walruses walk on all fours. However, like the earless seals, they have no ear flaps.

Robert E. Hynes

Leaving other herd members behind, a walrus roots for dinner along the sea bottom (above). This large pinniped eats as much as 100 pounds (45 kg) of shellfish a day.

Wall-to-wall walruses crowd a beach on Round Island, Alaska (left). Each summer, thousands of males land here. When winter comes, they rejoin the rest of the herd on chunks of floating ice.

15

Under its mother's gaze, a walrus calf learns to swim in the Bering Sea near Alaska. During lessons, a calf sometimes clings to its mother's flipper, or climbs onto her back. As the calf gains experience, it begins to swim on its own.

John J. Burns

Fluffy white coat of a harp seal pup keeps it warm and helps it hide from enemies in its arctic surroundings (above).

Life in icy seas

Several kinds of earless seals live in icy polar regions. But their living conditions are quite different. The ice of the Arctic is closely bordered by land. Polar bears, arctic foxes, and various birds kill many of these seals. Man has hunted them for centuries.

A vast area of ocean separates seals of the Antarctic from the nearest inhabited land to the north. Most of their predators are in the water. They have been little hunted by man. The waters they swim in support one of the world's richest food supplies. As a result, the antarctic seal population is very large. The crabeater seal alone numbers above 15 million—more than half the pinnipeds of the world.

Fred Bruemmer (top)   Norman R. Lightfoot/Nat'l Audubon Soc. Coll./P.R.

Coarse gray fur (above) replaces a month-old harp seal's white coat. Now the pup takes to the water in search of food.

18

Pilot Bud Christman carries a ribbon seal pup across ice on the Bering Sea. He is taking it to a helicopter for tagging and examination. Then he will let the pup go. If the pup is recaptured later, scientists will know how much it has grown and how far it has traveled.

John J. Burns

Seals live in icy areas at both ends of the earth. A leopard seal (above) sunbathes in antarctic waters. Its name comes from markings that resemble the spots of a leopard.

In northern waters, spots also mark the spotted seals seen in the large picture. These seals are resting and sunning on pieces of floating ice in an Alaskan bay.

20

Seal city! Northern fur seal males, females, and young crowd a rocky shore in Alaska's Pribilof Islands (left). In a rookery such as this, males watch over groups of females. The females care for the pups. Can you spot the young seals? They have velvety black coats. Below: A fur seal pup nurses. It depends on its mother for food for about four months; then it's on its own.

Leonard Lee Rue III/Nat'l Audubon Soc. Coll./P.R. (left)   Stephen J. Krasemann/DRK PHOTO

fur seal rookery

Every spring, northern fur seals travel to breeding grounds called rookeries. They crowd onto the shores of islands in the far north. Males arrive first. Each stakes out an area that will be his mating territory. A few weeks later, the females arrive.

Males take as many as 30 to 40 mates. Each female mates after giving birth to one pup. She takes care of the pup for about four months. Then she leaves the rookery until the following summer.

Rookeries are crowded and noisy. Females and males bark in greeting or in threat. Pups cry out constantly. By fall the rookery again is quiet; the herd has returned once more to feeding areas in the sea.

23

Gigi, a California sea lion, swims to trainer James E. Gray (above). He is handing her a bite plate attached to a line to be used in raising a Navy missile from the ocean floor.

On a training dive (right), Gigi attaches the line to a missile 40 feet (12 m) underwater. Next, crew members will reel in the line, drawing the missile to the water's surface.

Sea lions team up with the Navy

A test missile lies deep under the water. The United States Navy wants to get it back. How is it retrieved? Sometimes the Navy has the help of some well-trained sea mammals.

California sea lions are trained to dive to the sunken missile. A pinging sound from the missile guides the sea lion to the target. The animal, with the help of a bite plate, carries a line down from the surface. At the end of the line there is a special metal clip that snaps onto a U-shaped bolt on the missile. Navy crewmen aboard a ship then reel in the line and recover the missile. Sea lions have dived as deep as 350 feet (107 m) to do the job.

This recovery program is called Project Quick Find. Before it began in 1971, human divers in scuba gear had the task of finding sunken test missiles so they could be retrieved. Sea lions not only can dive deeper, but they also do the job faster, cheaper, and more safely.

Navy animal trainers teach each sea lion to perform certain actions. When the sea lion performs an action correctly, it receives a fish. It takes a sea lion up to a year to complete its training. During that time it learns to pull the line while diving, to find the missile by following the pinging sound, and to attach the line to the missile.

Once the sea lion's training is complete, it is ready to dive in the open ocean. It could easily swim away, but it doesn't. Its pay for the U. S. Navy job? . . . about 15 pounds (7 kg) of fish a day.

Mickey Pfleger (all)

Northern elephant seal pups rest together at Año Nuevo State Reserve in California (above). Born with dark coats, the pups molt, or shed their hair, when they are about six weeks old. Their new coats are silvery gray.

Año Nuevo elephant seals

On certain California beaches, enormous seals come ashore each year to bear their young, to molt, and to mate. Once these seals were nearly extinct because of overhunting for their blubber. Now the northern elephant seal is making a comeback.

During the 1950s, elephant seals started going ashore on Año Nuevo Island off California. Some years later they began to breed there. Now there are more than 2,000 animals in this herd.

Males go ashore first. They fight to see which ones will be the breeders. The largest weigh 5,000 pounds (2,268 kg), and are 16 feet (5 m) long. Later, the females arrive. Pups from last year's mating are born. Females mate again in about a month.

At Año Nuevo State Reserve, on the mainland near the island, visitors may take guided tours among the seals. But they must remember to keep a safe distance—at least 20 feet (6 m) away. The huge creatures can be dangerous.

WARNING WILD ELEPHANT SEALS STAY BACK 20 FEET

Looking for elephant seals along the far shore
of the reserve, a researcher is careful to keep a safe distance from the
group in front of her. The leader, a huge male, rests with his
mates and their pups. Each winter, northern elephant seals come
ashore here to bear their young and to mate.

Youngsters gaze at the huge bulk of a resting elephant seal (above). Mating season over, this male will soon return to the sea. Nearly extinct a century ago, northern elephant seals now number about 60,000.

Elephant seal molts, or sheds skin and hair, once a year. During this time, it lies on the beach and does not eat.

Why call this type of pinniped an elephant seal? This male's 14-inch (36-cm) nose should give you a clue (right)! Elephant seals also earn their name because they are the largest of the pinnipeds.

Lewis Trusty (large photograph)   Mickey Pfleger (above)

James Sugar (opposite and below)

🦭 *Six-month-old elephant seal opens wide for a fish (left). After being fed by hand, young seals at the California Marine Mammal Center must learn to catch their own fish before they can be released.*

🦭 *Dannie Butler and Pam Rogers use fish to coax two elephant seals into a tank (right). Recovering from illnesses, the seals practice swimming again before returning to the open sea.*

🦭 *Carma, a female elephant seal, scoots across a beach toward the ocean—and freedom (below). At the mammal center, she was cured of worms.*

Ilka Hartmann

Saving sea life

The California Marine Mammal Center, in Marin County near San Francisco, saves the lives of individual animals in trouble. When residents find an injured seal or sea lion, or come across an orphaned pup, they report the animal to the center. Staff members, helped by volunteers, go to the rescue.

After a sea mammal is brought in, a veterinarian examines it. If the animal is sick or hurt, it receives proper care. Orphans get careful attention to make sure they grow and thrive.

When an animal recovers, or grows big enough to take care of itself, staff members begin teaching it about life in the ocean. This means learning how to catch fish after being fed by hand. If all goes well, the animal is taken to the beach in a special cage. The door is opened, and the healthy animal makes its way to the ocean—to become a free sea mammal living among its own kind again.

31

Pinniped portrait gallery

Take a look at these faces. You'll see that pinnipeds come in many packages. Pinnipeds the world over have a lot of things in common. But there are also many differences among these sea mammals.

Whiskery walrus takes a dip off Alaska's Round Island (right). A walrus has about 400 whiskers on its face. It uses the bristles to feel for food on the ocean bottom.

ANIMALS ANIMALS/Z. Leszczynski

Stephen J. Krasemann/DRK PHOTO

Roberto Bunge/ARDEA LONDON

Sleek-snouted gray seals live in the North Atlantic (above). Canadians see them often. Some people call them horsehead seals because of the shape of their heads.

Gaping red mouth warns an intruder to keep away from a southern elephant seal (right). Accompanied by a loud noise, a display like this is usually enough to scare an enemy away from the seal.

Newborn bearded seal already has the full whiskers that give it its name (above). It is also born with a mask of light fur on its face. Later the mask will turn dark.

Thick hair covers the northern male fur seal (above). A fur seal's velvety undercoat averages 300,000 hairs to the square inch. No other pinniped wears a coat so thick.

2

Sea Otters

Lying on its back,
a sea otter floats comfortably
off the coast of California.
It rubs one arm with
the other to clean its fur.
A well-groomed coat traps air,
forming a thick covering that
keeps the animal warm.

Button-eyed sea otter peers from a bed of kelp off the coast of California. Kelp is a kind of seaweed. To maintain this alert position, the otter paddles with its hind feet much as a person treads water. Large lungs and a layer of air trapped in its thick fur help the animal float. To sleep and eat, the sea otter stretches on its back. It sometimes drapes itself with kelp to keep from drifting away.

Jeff Foott

Furry tool user: the sea otter

During the 1700s, Russian sailors exploring cold seas near Alaska saw thousands of furry sea otters. Hunters began traveling great distances to kill the animals for their fur. One report says that two hunters killed 5,000 in one year. Buyers in China paid high prices for the pelts.

Sea otters paid an even higher price. In less than two centuries, they were almost wiped out. In 1911, so few sea otters were left that the United States, Great Britain, Japan, and Russia signed a treaty limiting the number of otters that could be killed. This treaty, and laws that followed it, have allowed sea otters to make a comeback in the Pacific.

The thick fur that made the sea otter valuable to hunters helps the animal survive in chilly seas. The sea otter has no blubber. It has very thick fur. If kept in good condition, the fur readily traps air. The trapped air keeps the animal dry and warm. But if the coat becomes dirty and matted, there is no space for the air. The fur will soak up water. The animal will become wet and chilled and perhaps die.

A sea otter spends several hours a day caring for its fur. This process is called grooming. The animal frequently rolls over in the water to rinse bits of food from its coat. It also cleans its fur by rubbing it with its front paws. The water is removed by licking, squeezing, and rubbing the fur. Air can then move freely around the hairs, keeping the animal dry and warm.

Some sea otters live in the northern Pacific, off the coasts of Alaska and Russia. These northern animals sometimes go ashore to rest, to groom, and to

36

Side by side, a sea otter and her pup feed as they slowly swim. She stays close even after the pup is swimming on its own. They paddle with webbed hind feet. The drawing at left shows what a hind foot looks like. If you had a foot like a sea otter's, there would be webbing between your toes.

escape from storms. Other sea otters live along the central California coast. They do not go ashore as often as their northern relatives do.

Sea otters are well adapted to life in the water. Good swimmers, they push themselves through the water with webbed hind feet that act as flippers. They often swim on their backs with their heads out of the water.

Beds of kelp, a kind of seaweed, are rich feeding grounds for sea otters. They hunt such creatures as abalones, clams, and sea urchins. To get food, a sea otter dives and comes up with a shellfish. It also sometimes comes up with a rock to be used as a tool. The animal bobs on its back with the rock resting on its chest. If the sea otter has trouble opening the shellfish with its teeth or with its paws, it smashes it on the rock.

In this way, a sea otter eats as much as a fourth of its own weight every day. California fishermen blame the animals for shortages of abalone, a kind of sea snail prized as food by people as well as by sea otters. The fishermen think the animals should be kept in restricted areas. Other people think the sea otters should not be restricted at all.

For many, the California sea otter has become an educational attraction. People especially enjoy watching the mothers and their babies. The pups learn from their mothers how to swim, to hunt for food, and to use rocks as tools. Mothers and pups stay together for seven to nine months.

The sea otter still faces danger from oil slicks and pollution. But its story is amazing. In 1900, a person visiting California beaches would not have spotted a single sea otter. Today, it is not unusual to see rafts, or groups of 15 to 30 animals each, floating offshore in the kelp.

Sea cucumber, anyone? Swimming underwater, a sea otter holds a cucumber-shaped sea animal related to the starfish (left). An otter usually finds food in shallow water, but sometimes it goes as deep as 180 feet (55 m) or more. It stays down for about a minute and collects food with its front paws.

Crack! Using its chest as a table and a rock as a tool, a sea otter smashes open a clam. The otter has brought the rock up from the sea bottom for this purpose. In addition to the soft meat of clams, otters eat abalones, crabs, sea urchins, and fish. And they eat a lot! If a 100-pound (45-kg) person could eat as much compared to total size as a sea otter does, that person would be eating 25 pounds (11 kg) of food every day.

James A. Mattison, Jr., M.D. (above)   Jeff Foott (right)

Ron Kimball

Flip Nicklin (below, right, and opposite)

On the alert, a sea otter holds itself high in the water with paws outstretched (left). If startled, an otter takes this position, then dives underwater for safety.

Colored tags on the hind feet of otters help scientists identify them (above). The left foot tag identifies the individual animal. The right foot tag tells where the otter is from.

A biologist off the coast of California prepares to capture a sea otter. He holds a special net designed to catch one of the active animals. When the diver encircles an otter with the net he pulls a handle to draw the net tight. The captured otter gets colored identification tags and a physical exam. Then it is released. Since 1977, scientists have caught and tagged almost 300 sea otters in this part of the Pacific.

Tagging otters for science

A sea otter rests quietly at the surface of the ocean, stretched out on its back in a bed of seaweed. Suddenly a trap shaped like a large cup pops around it from below! A net closes, and the surprised sea otter is a captive.

But the hunter is not after the otter's fur. He is taking part in a program to tag sea otters along the California coast. He attaches color-coded plastic tags to the webbing of the hind feet of each otter he catches. After the animal is released, any researcher in the project who sees it will be able to identify it through binoculars or a telescope.

Scientists already have learned a lot from tagging. They now know that otters usually stay close to the place where they were tagged—eating, sleeping, and raising pups in one area.

Researchers have also learned more about the breeding patterns of sea otters. Observers of the tagged otters now believe the animals may have new pups every year, rather than every other year as previously thought.

Working from below, two divers try to catch a sea otter so it can be tagged for research. To capture the otter as it floats on the surface, they must push a net up through the seaweed.

3
Manatees

Man and manatee come
face to face in Florida's
Crystal River. Though
manatees have no known
natural enemies,
they usually shy away
from human beings. Some,
however, have seen divers
often enough to be more
curious than frightened.

Fred Bavendam

Gentle underwater grazer: the manatee

Christopher Columbus spotted manatees during his voyages to the New World. He noted in his ship's log that they were similar to creatures that had been identified elsewhere as mermaids. He was amused, for it is hard to see a resemblance between the blimp-shaped animal and a mythical woman with the tail of a fish.

There are three kinds of manatees. One kind lives in South America, in the Amazon River. Another lives along the Atlantic coast of Africa. A third kind, the West Indian manatee, lives in coastal waters around islands of the Caribbean Sea. It also is found along the southern shores of the Gulf of Mexico and in Florida.

In the United States in recent years, people have sighted manatees as far north as Virginia and as far west as Mississippi. But mostly the gentle mammals stay in Florida. Even there, they are barely holding their own. During the winter, the thousand or so manatees in Florida swim to the warmest water they can find. Manatees need warm water to survive because they have very little fat to keep them warm. Often they gather at warm springs or places where power plants discharge warm water.

Manatees have no known natural enemies. They live peaceful lives, swimming slowly through shallow fresh or salty waters, feeding on large amounts of water plants. Adults eat an average of 70 pounds (32 kg) of food a day.

Like all mammals, manatees breathe air. When they need air, they float just under the surface, poking their nostrils out of the water to take deep breaths. While they are swimming, manatees

Floating close to the surface of the water in Florida's Blue Spring State Park, a manatee munches a water hyacinth. It clutches the stem with its front flippers and uses its flexible upper lip to pull the plant into its mouth. A manatee spends six to eight hours a day eating all sorts of water plants. Because of its peaceful grazing habits, people sometimes call this marine mammal a sea cow. Manatees grow more than 12 feet (4 m) long and weigh as much as a ton.

44

Manatee, left, Steller's sea cow, center, and dugong, right, are brought together in a portrait. The artist put in a human diver for size. The huge sea cow has been extinct since the late 18th century, a victim of overhunting. The others survive, although in limited numbers.

breathe every three or four minutes. But when they are resting, they can stay underwater for as long as 15 minutes at a time.

A manatee easily cruises through the water at about 5 miles (8 km) an hour. If the animal is frightened, it swims faster, reaching speeds up to 15 miles (24 km) an hour for short distances. To swim, the manatee strokes its flattened tail in an up-and-down motion. It keeps its flippers close to its sides, occasionally using them to steer.

When in shallow water, a manatee uses its flippers to walk along the bottom. Nails on the tips of its flippers, and certain other characteristics, lead scientists to believe that the manatee is a distant relative of the elephant.

Manatees cruise alone, in pairs, or in small groups. Sometimes several come together to play. Cows and calves are the only manatees to have a long-term relationship. They stay together for as long as two years.

At birth, a manatee calf is only a little more than three feet (1 m) long. It weighs from 25 to 60 pounds (11 to 27 kg). Manatees do not have calves every year, the way some marine mammals do. A female bears one calf every two to three years.

It takes about one year for the baby to develop inside its mother's body. Scientists think that when the calf is born, its mother lifts it to the surface on her broad back. There, it takes its first breath. Soon after birth, the calf swims along at its mother's side. After a few months of nursing on rich milk, it begins to graze. For as long as two years, it continues to drink its mother's milk from time to time.

Manatee calves can be very playful, nuzzling and nibbling other manatees. Touch seems to be an important form of communication for all manatees. Adults nuzzle, nudge, and butt one another. Sometimes they even give each other hugs with their blunt front flippers.

Manatees are quiet and peaceful. They do not fight for food, nor do they attack other animals or people. Their only defense is to swim away from danger. Because of their peaceful ways, and because they graze in the water the way cows do on land, manatees are sometimes called sea cows.

The term "sea cow" is often used to describe an entire group of related sea mammals. Besides manatees, this group includes the dugong and the Steller's sea cow. Now extinct, the Steller's sea cow lived in the northern part of the Pacific Ocean. Early hunters of arctic foxes and sea otters killed the defenseless sea cows for meat until they were exterminated. The dugong survives in the coastal waters of the Indian Ocean and the western Pacific Ocean.

45

Side by side, a manatee mother and calf cruise underwater. Adults usually swim alone; only mothers and calves spend long periods of time together. The pairs stay close for about two years. Calves are often active and playful. Both young and old manatees sometimes hug each other with their flippers.

The manatee calf in the small picture at right may look as if it is trying to tickle its mother. But it's really nursing. A calf continues to drink the mother's rich milk for months after it has begun eating water plants. Born underwater, a manatee calf can swim soon after birth. Scientists think the mother lifts it to the surface on her back to take its first breath of air. After that, the calf surfaces by itself to breathe.

Fred Bavendam (both)

Ignoring a warning sign, a boater speeds out of a refuge area in Florida (above). Such carelessness can injure or kill manatees. A manatee hovers at the surface of the water as it breathes (right). Fast-moving boats would not have time to avoid the animal, nor could the manatee dive away in time to escape the sharp blades of whirling propellers. Speeding boaters who injure animals face big fines and possible jail sentences.

Jeff Foott (both)

Helping manatees survive

To breathe, manatees lie just beneath the surface of the water. From above, only the tips of their snouts can be seen. This way of breathing has become dangerous for manatees. Passing boaters may not spot the animals. They may pass right over a manatee, and cut it with the boat's propeller.

Many adult manatees that scientists have seen in Florida have propeller scars on their backs. In fact, the scars help identify individual animals. Injury and infection resulting from boating accidents are the leading causes of manatee deaths. Large boats sometimes kill manatees outright.

Can the problem be solved? Signs warn boaters to go slowly so as not to injure manatees and to avoid driving them away from warm water. The signs help, but they make another problem for the manatee at the same time.

Signs often attract people to manatee areas. Sport

48

Human hands help an orphan drink a special formula (right). This manatee was brought to Sea World of Florida when two weeks old. In eight months, it grew from 70 pounds to 200 pounds (32 to 91 kg).

Sport divers surround a manatee in a warm-spring area of Florida's Crystal River (right, below). Activity of this sort could drive the animal to colder water.

Propeller blades of a powerboat caused these scars on a manatee's back (below). Many manatees bear such scars.

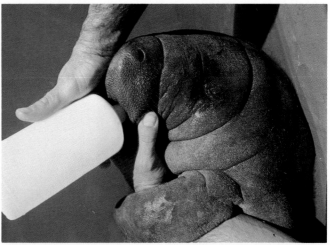

M. Timothy O'Keefe

Fred Bavendam

Jeff Foott

divers approach the animals to pet them or to take photographs. Although some manatees accept this attention, others swim away. Those driven off may swim into colder water to escape human beings. Because manatees have little fat, they cannot survive long if they stay in water below 68°F (20°C).

State and national laws now protect the animals in the United States. Certain warm-water areas in Florida have been set aside as refuges that restrict human contact with manatees. Heavy fines await

people who bother or hurt or kill the animals. At Blue Spring State Park, visitors watch manatees from platforms along a boardwalk. Only people with official permits may get into the water. And they must be careful not to frighten the manatees.

As part of the effort to maintain the population of the manatees, Florida has named the gentle mammal its official state marine mammal. The state is making efforts to teach the public about the manatee's special needs.

In Florida's Blue Spring State Park, researchers surround a manatee and place it on a stretcher. They will weigh and measure the mammal and fit a radio transmitter around its tail. Then they will release it.

Wearing a radio transmitter on its tail, a manatee swims in Florida. The radio sends out beeps. Researchers with receivers listen and track the manatee's movements.

Which way did they go? James Pertz uses a radio receiver to track manatees. When the antenna he holds points toward an animal with a transmitter, he hears loud beeps.

Tracing manatee travel

How do we know so much about where manatees usually swim? And where they feed? And when they move from place to place? How did we learn whether manatees swim together or travel alone? And how warm the water is where they live?

To answer questions such as these, scientists have placed radio transmitters on some manatees in Florida. The radios send beep signals to receivers in boats, on airplanes, or on shore. Each animal's radio has a different frequency. Listening to the signals, the scientists find out where the animals go, and when. They also can tell whether the manatees are swimming in warm or cold water. Beeps are slow in cold areas, but speed up in warm water.

Such information is important in helping people to preserve the manatee's habitat, or home. The more people know about the manatee, the more they will be able to help it survive.

Using its flipper, a manatee named Howie makes a playful grab for biologist Patrick Rose. Rose and other scientists are trying to learn more about how manatees live. They often dive in Howie's grazing area. Sometimes Howie seeks their attention, as he is doing here.

4
Mexico:
Whale Watch

Look out! Leaping from
the sea, a California gray whale
sends spray flying over
young whale watchers. Brett
Richardson, 12, and Ted
Gumerson, 11, both of
Oklahoma City, Oklahoma,
and Laura LewAllen, 16, of Santa Fe,
New Mexico, are part
of a whale-watching group off the
coast of Baja California,
in Mexico. "This whale loved to
play with us,"says Ted.
"It would swim away and hide,
then sneak up again right
beside us and squirt us with
mist from its blowhole!"

Whale watches whale watchers

*After a good look, a gray whale dives
near the whale watchers' ship, Mascot VI. Tail
flukes of gray whales may stretch
10 feet (3 m) across.*

What would it be like to see, touch, and play tag with a 50-foot whale! That's what Brett Richardson, 12, Ted Gumerson, 11, and Jack Markley, 13, all of Oklahoma, found out one February on a week-long adventure.

The boys joined 30 other people aboard a boat called *Mascot VI* at San Diego, California. Early in the morning, the boat headed south for warm waters off Baja California, in Mexico. Thousands of California gray whales go there every winter to mate and to have their young.

"On the first day, I saw sea gulls flying and lots of dolphins racing and jumping by our boat," said Brett. "Then, way out in the distance, I saw the spout of a whale. It looked like a fountain of spray. Pretty soon, we spotted whales blowing spouts in all directions around the boat. The whales made a kind of whooshing sound when they blew."

When *Mascot VI* reached San Ignacio Lagoon, the boys and the other passengers boarded inflatable rubber rafts to get closer to the whales. The operators told the passengers to be careful not to frighten or to disturb the animals.

"At first, the whales kept their distance," said Jack. "Then one whale came up and started following us. It was really friendly. We called it Queenie. It went to every raft and let the people pet it. A whale's skin feels like a wet leather basketball."

"Queenie really liked to play," Ted added. "Sometimes she would swim up under us and lift our raft up on her back. Or she would push us just a little with her snout and spin us around. Lots of times, she played tag. She would swim off, then come back and spray us through her blowhole!"

Between hours of whalewatching, the boys fished and went ashore on several islands to hike and to explore. "On one island, we saw a big herd of northern elephant seals with their babies," said Jack. "The huge seals were noisy and funny looking. Some of them were curious. They came right up to look at us."

"But the best part of the week was seeing whales up close," said Brett. "At first, I felt kind of scared because they were so huge. But then, I saw that they were really gentle and friendly. I think some of them liked us almost as much as we liked them!"

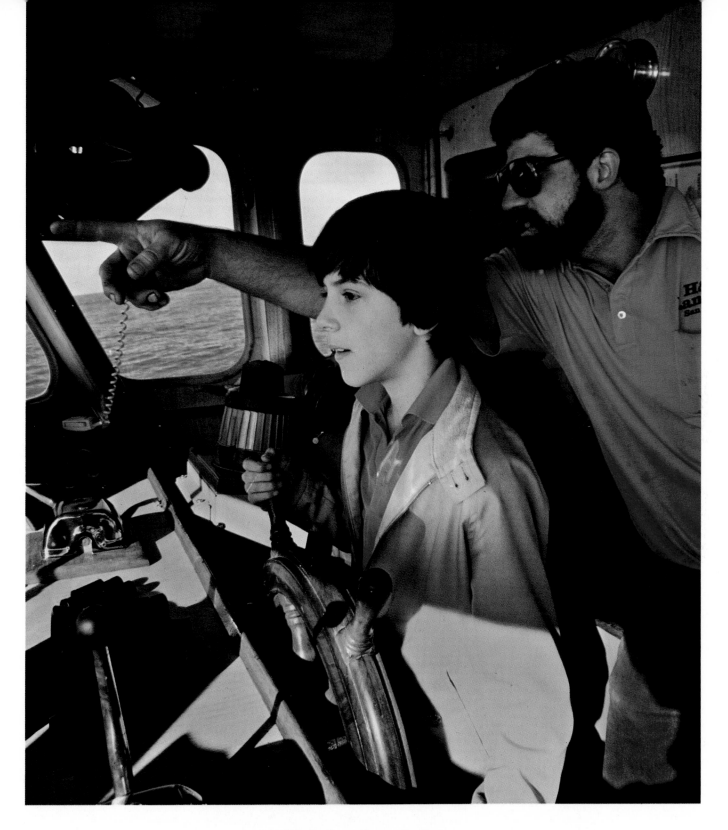

Sighting the whales

In the wheelhouse of Mascot VI, *Captain Bob Miller points
out the blow of a spouting whale to Jack Markley, 13, of Oklahoma City.
"On some days, we saw as many as 50 whales!" says Jack.*

Easy does it

Jack, Ted, and Brett relax in their rubber raft after a long day of whale watching in Mexican waters. The raft's motor had broken down, so the boys had to be towed back to Mascot VI. "We spent a lot of time in the raft watching the whales and fishing," says Jack. "By the end of each day, we were really tired and sunburned!"

Gentle giant

Swimming over to say hello, a curious gray whale bobs up beside a raft. Marcia Brice, center, and Marilyn Dudley reach out and urge it to come closer. Patches of skin on the whale's head are covered with barnacles and other small sea creatures.

"Mmm, that feels good"

Rising almost beneath another raft, a friendly whale seems to enjoy being petted by Jack, Brett, Ted, and Laura. "This whale was really affectionate," says Laura. "It stayed with us for about half an hour, then came back later. It even let me kiss it!"

Everybody out

Beaching their raft on a deserted island, Brett, right, and other passengers jump ashore to explore. "While looking for harbor seals and western gulls, we saw a lot of interesting plants and shells," says Brett.

Treetop lookout

On another island, the boys perch in an elephant tree (left). The branches of this desert tree look a little like elephants' trunks.

Look at that nose!

Jack, Ted, and Brett cautiously approach a huge male elephant seal. Its nose resembles an elephant's trunk. "That seal was really big," says Ted. "When he turned around and bellowed at us, we took off fast!"

59

Heading for home

*As **Mascot VI** gets under way, Jack, Brett, and Ted watch the sun go down over the water. "It was sad leaving our friends the whales," says Jack. "Even at night you could hear them blowing. I hope we can come back next year."*

Pacific postal service

Near the end of the trip, Jack and Ted seal notes in bottles (left) to throw into the sea. "Maybe someone will find our bottles and write back to us," says Ted.

5
Toothed Whales

Swimming in a group called a pod, four spotted dolphins hunt for fish and other prey. Dolphins are actually whales. They belong to a large group known as toothed whales. Most toothed whales, including dolphins, have cone-shaped teeth. They use the teeth to catch and to hold prey. A hitchhiking fish called a remora clings to the underside of the dolphin at the top.

Strong teeth
for hunting in the sea

For centuries, whales have been among the most familiar of the marine mammals. People are learning more about them all the time.

Whales fit into two groups: those with teeth, such as the one shown at the right; and those without teeth, described in the next chapter.

We tend to think of the great whales in general as being toothless creatures, yet of the more than 75 species of whales, at least 65 have teeth. Toothed whales range in size from 5-foot (2-m) dolphins, or porpoises, to 55-foot (17-m) great sperm whales. People often use the words dolphin and porpoise to refer to the same animal. Most toothed whales eat fish, squid, and shellfish. They use their cone-shaped teeth to grab and to hold prey. But they don't chew their food. They swallow it whole.

Whales live in all the oceans of the world. A great many of them are found in the cold waters of the Arctic. These mammals are well equipped for living in icy seas. Each has a thick layer of fat, called blubber, to keep it warm.

The bodies of whales are smooth and torpedo-shaped to help them glide through the water. In spite of their size, whales twist, turn, and dive with speed and ease. A whale has two large fins, called flukes, at the end of its tail. It pushes itself through the water with the flukes, using an up-and-down movement of its tail.

Whales use the flippers on their sides for steering. Many of them also have fins on their backs, called dorsal fins. These provide balance.

A toothed whale breathes through a blowhole, a kind of nostril, on the top of its head. When a whale surfaces to breathe, it shoots, or blows out, all the air in its lungs. The whale's warm breath hits the cooler

Tom Stack/TOM STACK & ASSOCIATES

Opening its powerful jaws, a killer whale shows strong, cone-shaped teeth. Like most toothed whales, the killer whale uses its teeth to catch many kinds of prey. It hunts fish, seals, and even other whales. Its teeth curve slightly inward and grip the prey. The whale swallows without chewing.

air and forms a cloud of mist. This action is known as the "blow" of the whale. It is very much like seeing your own breath on a cold day.

Then the whale inhales fresh air. After breathing in, the whale closes its blowhole with a strong muscle. This muscle keeps water from entering the blowhole when the whale dives again.

From every few seconds to an hour or more whales come to the surface to breathe. They stay down longest when being pursued. Sperm whales probably dive deeper than any other kind of whale. They plunge a half-mile or more to find squids, one of their favorite foods. When a whale at the surface dives deep, the action is called sounding.

Sperm whales, like most toothed whales, use echolocation (say ek-oh-low-KAY-shun) to find their food. As the mammals swim underwater, they send out high-pitched clicking sounds. The echoes of these sounds help the whales locate prey (see pages 74-75).

These sounds probably also help whales to communicate with each other. In addition to clicking noises, toothed whales send out chirps, squeaks, whistles, and low moaning groans. Sound travels well underwater, so whales may communicate over a distance of hundreds or even thousands of miles. No one really knows how far their sounds travel.

Most toothed whales travel in pods. Some dolphins swim in pods of a hundred or more. They are very active in the water. They can be seen leaping and splashing and swimming along with ships. Sometimes they ride on the high waves at the front of a ship.

Swimming on the surface of the sea, dolphins move with an easy rolling motion. They leap out of the water to breathe, then they dive gracefully back into the sea again.

Some experts believe that dolphins are among the most intelligent and sociable of all whales. They are also protective of one another. People at sea have seen dolphins and other whales helping a sick or injured comrade.

Dolphins and other toothed whales have few natural enemies except for sharks. Younger or weaker whales often fall victim to sharks. Studies show that sharks also attack large, healthy whales.

Strangely enough, the killer whale, the largest of the dolphins, is a deadly enemy to all the other whales. It cuts through the water at speeds as high as 30 miles (48 km) an hour when pursuing prey. Scientists think killer whales may be able to see well both above and below the surface of the water.

Like the larger whales, killer whales have been seen breaching, or leaping high out of the sea. Or they may push their heads straight up out of the water, an action called spy-hopping. It is not known what meaning these actions have, but they may serve as communication signals among killer whales while they are hunting.

Killer whales hunt in packs of as many as 40, much as wolves do on land. In fact, Eskimos call these whales "wolves of the sea." Working together, killer whales go after seals and encircle and attack even the largest whales.

Ancient Romans called the killer whale the *orca*, or "sea devil." Its present name came from whaling men much later. Whalers saw these swift black-and-white whales attacking other whales much larger than themselves. In some cases, a whaling crew was able to locate large whales because killer whales had already encircled them. As a result, the men called this animal the "whale killer." Eventually, the name became reversed to "killer whale."

The killer whale seems to deserve its name. Though familiar to thousands as the friendly star of marine shows, it is anything but friendly in the wild. Its purpose in killing is probably to feed, but people have often seen it kill without eating a bite.

Wild and tame killer whales

Although killer whales are aggressive hunters in their natural surroundings, they are surprisingly gentle and playful in captivity. Since the 1960s, many have been captured and trained to perform tricks in aquariums. Some of these mammals learn to leap high for fish and to jump over barriers above water on command. They seem to become attached to their human trainers, and are willing to give them rides on their backs. There is no record of a killer whale in the wild attacking a human being.

Norman Tomalin/Bruce Coleman Inc.

Ken Balcomb (below and right)

Leaping high, a killer whale responds to a trainer's whistle at Sea World of Florida (top). Killer whales are easily trained in captivity. Most of the tricks they perform are actually variations of natural behavior they follow in the wild. Above: A killer whale breaches, or leaps out of the water, off the coast of Washington.

Tall fin on the back of a killer whale rises above the water. These fins, up to 6 feet (2 m) tall, resemble the fins of sharks.

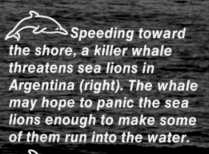

Speeding toward the shore, a killer whale threatens sea lions in Argentina (right). The whale may hope to panic the sea lions enough to make some of them run into the water.

Pod of killer whales attacks a great blue whale (below). After ripping chunks from its huge body, they let it swim away.

Killer whales use many tricks to earn their meals (left). This young seal on floating ice in antarctic waters is not safe. In such a situation, killer whales swim toward the ice, make a large wave, and wash the victim into the sea.

Dolphins swim off the coast of California (below). Certain dolphins are often found near schools of tuna, and many are caught in the nets of tuna fishermen. United States fishermen have developed ways to save most of the dolphins trapped in tuna nets.

Gerard M. Wellington

Joseph A. Thompson, Seavision Productions (above and right)

Crewman from a tuna boat searches for dolphins caught in the boat's net (right). He and other men in rubber rafts and speedboats chase dolphins to a point at the end of the net farthest from the tuna boat.

Helping to save dolphins in danger

For some reason unknown to humans, large schools of tuna fish often are found along with groups of dolphins. The fish swim just below the dolphins.

It did not take tuna fishermen long to learn this. When they began using nets, they set the nets in large circles around groups of dolphins.

The fishermen found that by using this method they caught many more tuna. But they also trapped hundreds of dolphins each time they set their nets. The dolphins often became confused and panicky. Many suffocated before the fishermen could release them from their nets.

Then, in 1972, the United States government passed a law called the Marine Mammal Protection Act. The act made it illegal, with certain exceptions, to trap or to kill dolphins. American tuna fishermen immediately started developing ways to save dolphins trapped in the nets.

Today, a tuna boat captain sends out men in small speedboats to watch for dolphins caught in the net. These men chase the dolphins to the far end of the net, away from the side of the tuna boat.

Then the captain reverses engines and moves his tuna boat backward. This lets the back edge of the net sink below the surface near the dolphins. The dolphins can then swim free while the tuna remain trapped in the net.

Men in rubber rafts also help the dolphins by chasing them to the escape area. In 1980, these methods saved all but 15,000 of the dolphins caught in tuna nets. This compares with 350,000 dolphins accidentally killed in 1972, the year the Marine Mammal Protection Act was passed. Fishermen and government officials are proud of this record.

Working underwater during a special research cruise, a diver pushes a dolphin out of the net by hand (right). This is not common practice, because of danger from sharks that might be trapped in the net. On a regular tuna run, divers do not go into the water.

🐬 *Duffy, a bottlenose dolphin, leaps high out of the water to catch a ball (left). Duffy is responding to a signal from Mandy Rodriguez. He and other trainers at Flipper's Sea School in Florida are developing a whistle vocabulary to communicate with dolphins.*

🐬 *Good friends: Natua the dolphin and Mandy the trainer swim together (left).*

🐬 *A dolphin named Delphi poses for trainer Lynne Calero (below). In the wild, dolphins would not leave the water as this task requires.*

Unlocking secrets of dolphin communication

Just how smart are dolphins? No one knows for sure. Some people think they are very smart indeed.

For years, people have known that dolphins communicate with each other by making a variety of sounds, including whistles, squeaks, and clicks. No one knows what these sounds mean. But some scientists think dolphins have a language as useful as that of humans.

At Flipper's Sea School, in Grassy Key, Florida, researchers are studying dolphin communication. They have even developed a whistle vocabulary so they can "talk" to the dolphins. They want to find

73

out whether dolphins can understand and respond to various commands given by trainers in this language of whistles.

The sea school has 16 Atlantic bottlenose dolphins. They range in age from 2½-year-old Rosetta to 30-year-old Mr. Gippy. Some of the animals are trained to give shows for the public. In the shows, the dolphins demonstrate their intelligence and physical abilities by performing tasks. These include leaping through hoops, shooting basketballs through nets, and walking backward across the water on their tails.

Other dolphins are not shown to the public, but are used only in the school's dolphin language research program.

Mandy Rodriguez is director of training and co-director of research at Flipper's. For three and a half years, he and other trainers have been developing a whistle vocabulary to test the dolphins' intelligence. How does it work?

"We now have about ten 'words,' or whistle cues, that the dolphins understand," says Mandy, "words like 'jump,' 'dive,' 'touch,' and 'rock.'"

The trainers use their mouths to whistle the cues into a microphone. The microphone sends the sounds underwater to the dolphins. When the

"You're doing great! Keep it up." That's what trainer Carol Smith's hand signal and smile tell a dolphin named Longnose (below). Longnose holds a ball in her flippers while she walks across the water on her tail. Dolphins are rewarded with fish when they perform well. But a trainer's affection, applause, and warm smile also provide encouragement for the mammals.

Matt Herron (left)   N.G.S. Photographer Joseph H. Bailey

Whistling into a microphone, Mandy asks Natua to find an object underwater (left). The dolphin is blindfolded with soft eye cups. If Natua correctly understands the whistle request, he will use echolocation to locate the right object.

dolphins hear the whistles, they perform certain tasks such as touching objects underwater.

Trainers also use whistle sounds for each dolphin's name. By whistling the name for a dolphin, such as Natua, and adding a series of word cues, the trainers can ask a specific dolphin to do a certain task. For example, a trainer might whistle a combination like this: "Natua—dive—touch—rock."

The dolphins are tested over and over again to see whether they respond to the whistled cues and perform correctly.

Researchers use computers to help them study the results of these tests. In time, the researchers hope to show that dolphins do have the ability to learn a language.

"If we can prove without doubt that these animals are highly intelligent, thinking beings," says Mandy, "perhaps we can make people more anxious to save and to protect them."

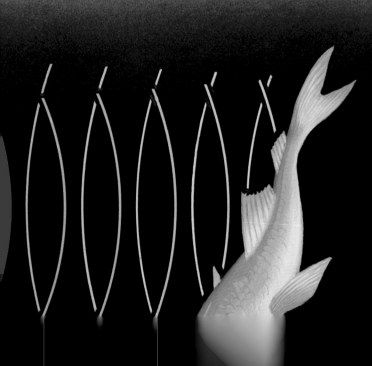

Dolphins have good eyesight, but echoes help them locate things they cannot see. This ability is called echolocation. The drawing shows how echolocation works. As the dolphin swims, it sends out high-pitched clicking noises. Scientists now know that these noises come from air spaces inside the front of the dolphin's head. When the noises hit an object, such as a fish, echoes bounce back. By listening to the echoes, the dolphin can tell the direction of the object, how far away it is, and if it is moving. The echoes also tell the dolphin the size and shape of the object. Dolphins use these signals to find food and to escape enemies. Echolocation works so well that a dolphin swimming in a large tank, with its eyes covered, can locate a target the size of a quarter!

Laura Ground, 10, left, and her sister, Leslie, 13, watch Mandy check Natua's teeth (above). Living near Flipper's Sea School, the girls knew the dolphins well and played with them often. Play sessions are needed, says Mandy, to keep dolphins from being bored.

The Ground sisters learn more about dolphins from trainer Belle Benson Lyons (right). She injects water into fish to be fed to Mr. Gippy, left, and Little-Bit. The added moisture helps dolphins that are slightly ill.

Baleen Whales

Whale of a surprise! As young adventurers paddle their kayak in Prince William Sound, Alaska, a humpback whale suddenly dives right beside them. Although it came close enough to splash their boat, the kayakers felt no danger. Humpback whales belong to a group of sea animals known as baleen whales.

Mighty giants of the deep

Of all the animals that live in the sea, by far the largest are the whales called baleen (say buh-LEEN) whales. Some baleen whales are the biggest animals that have ever lived. One kind, the blue whale, grows nearly 100 feet (30 m) long and weighs more than 130 tons (118 t). That's 30 times as heavy as an average African elephant.

Oddly enough, these gigantic whales feed mainly on tiny animals. The animals, called krill, resemble small shrimp. Baleen whales do not have teeth to catch food. They have comblike plates called baleen suspended from their upper jaws. The baleen acts as a huge strainer.

To eat, a baleen whale takes in water as it swims. When it has a mouthful, the whale closes its jaws and forces the water out through the baleen. The krill remains trapped behind the baleen. The whale then swallows the food. Some whales eat enormous amounts of krill. An adult blue whale may eat four tons a day.

Baleen is sometimes called whalebone, but it is not really bone. It is a strong, flexible material much like that of your fingernails. The size and shape of the baleen varies from one type of whale to another. Baleen plates of the gray whale are only about 18 inches (46 cm) long. But those of the bowhead whale may grow as long as 14 feet (4 m).

During the summer, most baleen whales feed in the cold waters of the polar regions. There, krill and other tiny animals are so numerous that they can make the sea look like a thick soup.

One whale, the humpback, has an unusual way of feeding. It sometimes herds large amounts of krill and small fish together by blowing bubbles that act as a net. First, the whale dives deep. Then it turns and begins to swim upward, going around and around in circles. At the same time, it blows bubbles through its blowholes. The circles of bubbles form a net that forces the krill and fish together and up to the surface. Then the whale swims up through the middle of the bubble net with its jaws open wide and scoops up its catch!

The humpback whale is not really humpbacked at all. Its name comes from the way it exposes a large part of its back when diving. It seems to arch its back, giving it a humped appearance.

During the summer, most baleen whales spend their time feeding. They may gain as much as 40 tons (36 t) of blubber. Then they migrate long distances to warmer waters for the winter. During these journeys, the whales eat very little. They live off their blubber.

California gray whales migrate about 5,000 miles (8,047 km) from their feeding grounds off Alaska's coast to their winter homes in waters near Mexico. The trip takes about 4 months of almost nonstop swimming. Scientists do not know how the whales find their way. But every year, without maps or compasses, they follow the same paths.

When they arrive in warmer waters, the females are pregnant. They give birth, then later mate again. Their babies are called calves. Most are born tail-first, and must surface immediately to breathe. Mothers may help their babies by pushing them quickly to the surface.

Young whales grow fast. A blue whale comes into the world weighing about 2 tons. Some scientists believe it drinks more than 50 gallons (189 l) of its mother's milk a day. This milk is very rich in fat, and the baby grows about 8½ pounds (4 kg) an hour during the first 7 months of its life.

The blue whale is the largest of all the whales. It is powerful almost beyond belief. One story tells about a blue whale that was harpooned by whalers

Skimming the Atlantic Ocean with an open mouth, a right whale feeds (above). Two rows of whalebone plates called baleen hang down like giant combs from the whale's top jaw. The whale eats tiny animals that the baleen filters from the water.

Hardly bigger than a man's thumb, shrimplike creatures called krill float in the ocean (left). Baleen whales feed mainly on krill. It takes more than a ton of these animals to fill a large whale's stomach.

aboard a steam-powered ship 90 feet (27 m) long. The wounded whale towed the ship for nearly 24 hours before it finally died. During the entire time, the crew kept the ship's engines running in reverse!

Yet in spite of their great size and strength, some baleen whales behave in ways that appear to be playful. Even adult baleen whales seem to enjoy active playing. The humpback is one of the most active and acrobatic of all whales. Humpbacks are often seen leaping out of the sea and splashing back in. This is called breaching. The 40-ton whales may repeat the performance 20 times in a row. If there were a whale Olympics, a humpback would probably win the gold medal.

Apparently, all baleen whales make sounds to communicate underwater. Scientists have eavesdropped on some of these whale conversations with underwater microphones. The most remarkable sounds are the haunting songs of the humpback whale. These whales make whistling, wailing, and sighing sounds and repeat them over and over.

No one knows all the reasons why these whales sing. It may be to exchange information about feeding or migrations. Or it may be a way for them to keep in touch with each other across miles of ocean.

Scientists believe that some baleen whales live as long as 80 years. But, since American deep-sea whaling began almost 300 years ago, many of these gentle giants have met early deaths. Whalers hunted the animals for their oil, meat, and baleen. In 1930, whalers caught almost 30,000 blue whales alone. By 1965, they could find fewer than 400.

Today the blue whale and other species in various parts of the world are in danger of dying out. The United States and many other nations are trying to see that this does not happen. They have passed laws and signed agreements limiting the hunting of whales. Some have established refuges, or protected areas, for whales.

In 1972, the Mexican government established a national whale refuge off Baja California where gray whales have their young. And in 1974, the government of Argentina set aside an area off its coast to protect the breeding grounds of right whales.

The Marine Mammal Protection Act of 1972 committed the United States to the protection of marine mammals. With certain exceptions, the law makes it illegal for citizens to kill these animals. It also closes U. S. borders to products from sea mammals killed by people living in nations that still allow hunting.

The United States continues to push for a worldwide ban on all commercial whaling.

Ed Robinson (both)

Like all baleen whales, the humpback (above) has two blowholes on top of its head. Small bumps of a kind seen on no other whale cover the head.

Lift-off! A humpback whale leaps out of the Pacific Ocean near the Hawaiian Islands. This action is called breaching. The humpback is one of the most acrobatic of the whales. It often rolls

over in the air and lands on its back
with a splash. Flippers help the whale push
itself from the water. Some flippers are more
than 14 feet (4 m) long.

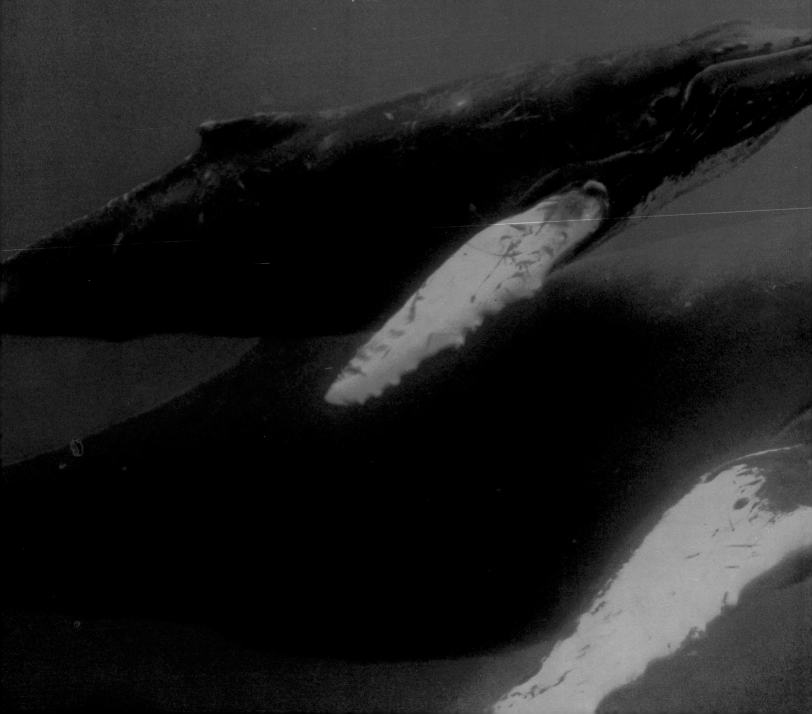

In clear Pacific waters, a humpback whale swims up and looks at photographer Chuck Nicklin (right). Curious and friendly, humpbacks are also playful. They often leap out of the water and slap it with their long flippers.

Flip Nicklin

Francoise Gohier/ARDEA LONDON   Graeme Ellis, Nanaimo, B.C. (large photograph)

Diving over its mother's back, a baby gray whale plays in the warm ocean (left). After several months, they will migrate 5,000 miles (8,047km) to arctic feeding grounds.

Humpback whale baby glides above its mother (below). For nearly a year it will drink her rich milk —and grow and grow!

Whales with crusty heads

Right whales, like the one above, are born with rough patches on their heads. These are called callosities (say kuh-LAH-sih-teas). They are actually raised areas of tough, thickened skin.

No two individuals have callosities exactly alike.

Some whales have growths that look like crusty eyebrows, mustaches, beards, or even sideburns. Most have at least one large callosity on the top of the head. This was called a bonnet by old-time whalers because they thought it looked somewhat like a woman's hat of the 19th century.

In what appears to be an aggressive act, a whale

Unforgettable face belongs to a right whale (left). Only the right whale has patches of rough skin like these. They are called callosities. No one knows everything about callosities, but it is known that tiny animals such as the ones below live in them.

Scott D. Kraus/New England Aquarium

Jeff Foott

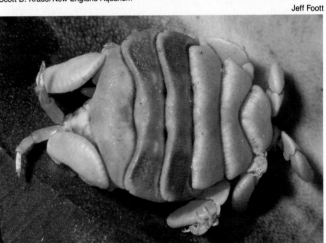

Des and Jen Bartlett

sometimes rubs its rough bonnet across the back of another whale. Scientists are studying what other uses callosities might have.

The right whale was named by early whalers who considered it the "right" whale to hunt. It swims slowly, does not sink when it dies, and provides large amounts of oil and baleen.

Getting a free ride, animals such as barnacles anchor themselves to the crusty callosities of right whales and to the skin of gray whales and humpbacks (top picture). To keep from slipping off as the whale swims, the whale louse (above) takes shelter among the barnacles. This picture shows a louse several times its actual size. The louse feeds on the whale's flaking skin.

Hunting the whales

For centuries, people hunted whales for meat, oil, and baleen. In the 19th century, whaling was a major industry in the United States. During that time, hundreds of whaling ships sailed from Nantucket and New Bedford, in Massachusetts, and from other eastern ports. On voyages that often lasted for years, the whalers hunted baleen whales and also the large sperm whales.

When the ship's lookout sighted the spout of a whale, he cried "Thar she blows!" Small whaling boats were quickly lowered into the sea, and the chase began. The men rowed furiously to get close enough to the whale for the harpooner to spear it.

Harpooning was a dangerous business. Sometimes the uncoiling harpoon line caught around a man's arm or leg and yanked it off, or pulled the harpooner overboard. Once the line became tight, the wounded whale would pull the tiny boat behind it on a mad race across the waves. Whaling men called this ride a "Nantucket sleighride."

Even after the whale tired, there were dangers. An exhausted whale could still smash a boat with its tail flukes as it lashed about.

Once the whale died, it was towed back to the ship. Its blubber was cut off and boiled down into oil. This oil was sold to burn in lamps and to be made into candles, soap, and lubricants.

Later in the history of American whaling, baleen whales faster than bowhead and right whales were hunted. The baleen was cut out of the whale's mouth and stored in the ship. The tough baleen was used to make such things as umbrella ribs, buggy whips, clock springs, and corsets. Baleen became a more valuable whale product than oil.

Today, substitutes can be found for many whale products. But the needs of some nations cause them to continue to hunt whales for meat and oil.

The picture above, painted in 1833, shows a sperm whale hunt in waters near the Hawaiian Islands. Risking death, sailors harpoon the whales from small, open boats. In the foreground, a crew finishes killing a wounded whale. A whaler drives his harpoon into the animal's side while his mates steer the boat. Why were whales killed? In the days before people knew how to pump oil out of the ground, the blubber of sperm whales provided most of the oil for Europe and the United States. Whale oil kept lamps burning and machinery greased.

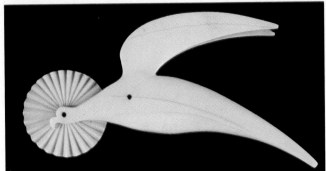

On long voyages, whalers carved designs on the teeth and jawbones of sperm whales. They called their work scrimshaw. The scrimshaw bird above decorates a pie-crust trimmer.

Fishermen stop by the body of a fin whale that washed ashore in the Province of Quebec, in Canada. It may have died of natural causes, or possibly from suffocation in a fish net. Whales normally have about the same life span as that of human beings.

Russ Kinne/Nat'l Audubon Soc. Coll./P.R.

Ron Church

Bones of a gray whale (above) whiten in the sun on a beach in Mexico. By studying beached whales, scientists gain knowledge that helps them understand a worldwide but still little known form of life.

Helping hands. Alan Birse, left, Tim Green, and Steve Waller, right, free a baby gray whale stranded on a sandbar in Mexico. It swam back to sea. Strandings happen in the shallow bays of Baja California for various reasons. Calves of gray whales sometimes become separated from their mothers. Or sometimes a calf may be born weak or sickly and drift helplessly to shore.

C. Allan Morgan

People helping whales

For unknown reasons, toothed whales as well as the baleen whales sometimes become stranded on beaches. Many stranded whales cannot help themselves and do not live long.

On April 15, 1981, a young sperm whale became stranded at Coney Island, New York. Biologists discovered the whale had pneumonia. They named it Physty (say FY-stee) and treated it with antibiotics.

Physty seemed to recover and was pushed gently out to sea. Some people thought Physty might want to stay. But as thousands cheered, the whale turned to the sea and swam away.

7

Hawaii:

Sea Life
Park

Heads up! Under a blazing
sun on Oahu Island in Hawaii,
two bottlenose dolphins
tailwalk across Whaler's Cove,
part of Sea Life Park. The
dolphins are named Mikioi and
Kaleo. They perform this trick
three times a day. Look closely at
the picture. You'll see the
dolphins' trainer standing at the
edge of the cove. The trainer's
raised arm is a signal to the
animals. They rear up and
splash all the way across the
pool, using their strong tails
to push themselves along.

Photographs in this chapter by Richard A. Cooke III

Stopping by to Say Aloha

Two Atlantic bottlenose dolphins greet trainer Cindy Cookingham as she paddles an outrigger canoe in Whaler's Cove. She will drape them with necklaces of flowers called leis.

Tom Stack/TOM STACK & ASSOCIATES

Shiny black forms swim through the water on the island of Oahu, in the state of Hawaii. Suddenly, two large sleek bodies burst through the surface of Whaler's Cove. Makapuu and I'anui make startling side-by-side leaps over a rope. This is your watery welcome to Sea Life Park.

Makapuu and I'anui are false killer whales. They have been trained to do tricks. Each one weighs about 1,200 pounds (544 kg). They differ in size and shape from true killer whales and they are black all over, instead of black and white.

For years, Makapuu and I'anui have been star performers in the shows at Whaler's Cove, one of the main attractions of Sea Life Park. There, a huge tank that looks like a cove of the Pacific Ocean is the scene of three splashy shows every day.

You will learn a lot about marine mammals if you visit the park. You will also have fun! Perhaps you will feed a fish to a sea lion at the feeding pool and be rewarded with a trick. Remember, though, feed them only what the keepers give you. Don't toss any coins into their pool. This can cause poisoning if the animals swallow them.

You can watch training demonstrations at the Ocean Science Theater. There, trainers work with dolphins and sea lions, teaching them tricks to do in the shows. The trainers also have taught the dolphins to help divers in the open sea by bringing back tools, by carrying messages to the surface, and even by rescuing human divers who have been injured.

At Whaler's Cove you can see the results of the special training that is needed to teach huge mammals like Makapuu and I'anui to leap across a rope above the water. All these animals learn by means of a reward system. When they obey commands they receive fish, words of praise, pats on the head, or play periods. When they make mistakes, they get nothing.

There are many other attractions at Sea Life Park that give people a chance to become better acquainted with animals that live in the sea. While visitors are enjoying these creatures they are also learning more about them.

How do places like Sea Life Park get their marine mammals? They must have permits to capture these animals in the wild. Whenever possible, they use animals that have been rescued from illness or injury and brought back to health.

Leaping for Lunch

Pacific bottlenose dolphin leaps about 20 feet (6 m) above the surface. This leap almost doubles the height a dolphin would normally leap in the wild. A fresh fish is the reward.

Bareback Ride Over the Waters

Holding tight to a hoop around the body of Makapuu, a false killer whale, Cindy rides across Whaler's Cove. Makapuu has been a star performer at Sea Life Park since 1965. The animal always receives a reward when it performs correctly. It is never punished or scolded for failure; it simply gets no reward.

Up and Over

At exactly the same moment, two false killer whales burst from the water and leap in opposite directions over a rope. How do they know when to jump? The two animals, Makapuu and I'anui, hear a signal. Their trainer sends a sound through an underwater speaker—and the animals take off.

Reward for a Good Show

After their show, Makapuu and I'anui open wide to accept handfuls of fish from assistant curator of mammals Diana Wong. As a trainer, Diana strengthens her bonds with the animals by feeding them herself. If they do not perform correctly, Diana just tries again another time. Such training takes patience. But false killer whales are quick to learn—and to earn rewards.

97

Balancing Act

Opihi, a California sea lion, balances a ball on its nose during a show at the Ocean Science Theater. This looks easy, but balancing isn't part of a sea lion's natural behavior. It's a hard trick to learn, but Opihi needed only a few weeks.

Surrounded by Sea Lions

In the feeding pool, trainer Jon Lauterbach hands out fish to some of the 45 California sea lions living at Sea Life Park. Depending on their size, these sea lions eat from 7 to 20 pounds (3 to 9 kg) of fish each day. The park's sea lion population is always growing. Several babies are born each year.

Hoisting a Dolphin

Student volunteer Jason Swartz, 15, keeps a dolphin calm as it is raised from the water for a medical exam. As a Sea Life Park volunteer, Jason spends two days a week helping to care for the marine mammals. Jason hopes to work full time at the park after finishing school.

Marine Medical Exam

Jason helps Ingrid Kang, curator of mammals at Sea Life Park, prepare a dolphin for a checkup. Diana stands ready to assist. Regular medical checkups are part of the routine at Sea Life Park. Dolphins receive checkups twice a year. Staff members weigh and vaccinate them and give them blood tests. They inspect each dolphin for injuries, then return it to the water.

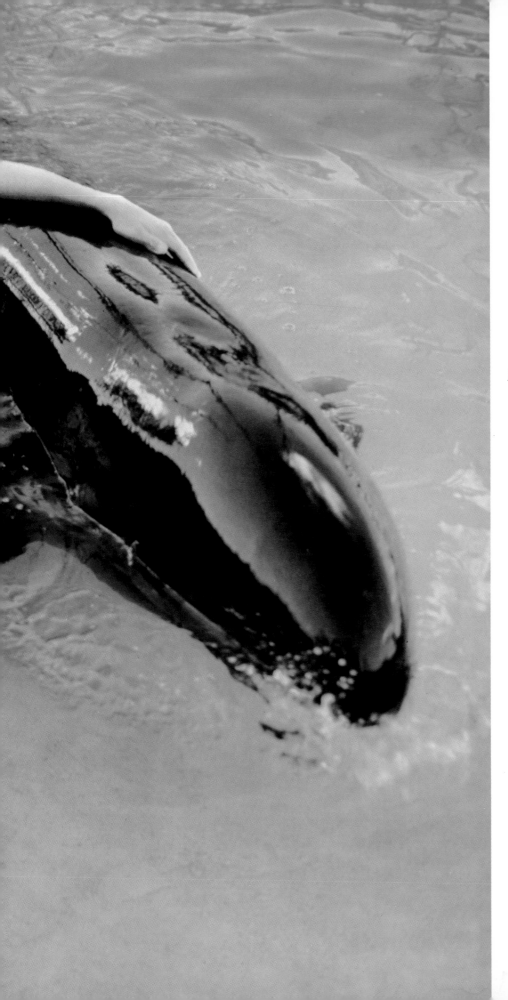

Whale of a Time

Taking a break from his volunteer job, Jason makes friends with two false killer whales. Jason admits being "a little bit scared" the first time he swam with I'anui, left, and Makapuu. For safety's sake, the animals' trainers stayed nearby. The whales are very friendly, the trainers say. But they're also large and powerful, so they must be handled with care and respect.

Glossary

baleen—plates in the upper jaw of some whales that strain out the small animals the whale eats

barnacle—small shellfish that attaches itself to underwater objects and to whales

blowhole—nostril at the top of a whale's head through which it breathes (Some whales have two blowholes.)

blubber—layer of fat under the skin of most marine mammals

breaching—action in which a whale leaps out of the water

callosities—patches of thick, rough skin on the heads of right whales

echolocation—method used by some whales to find their way underwater by sending out sounds and listening to the echoes

endangered—reduced to the point of being nearly extinct

extinct—no longer in existence

flukes—flattened parts of a whale's tail

grooming—the action of an animal in keeping itself clean

krill—small shellfish that are the main food source of many baleen whales

lobtailing—repeated action in which a whale raises its tail high into the air and slaps it down on the water

mammal—any animal that breathes air, has some kind of hair, is warm-blooded, gives birth to live young, and lives on mother's milk when young

marine—relating to the sea

molting—shedding of an animal's hair and sometimes skin

orca—another name by which the killer whale is known

pod—name for a group of whales that travel together

porpoise—small toothed whale (This word is often used interchangeably with dolphin.)

rookery—place on shore where some pinnipeds go to mate, to give birth, and to raise young

scrimshaw—carving done on bones and teeth of sea mammals

shellfish—any of several kinds of small, shelled marine animals

sounding—deep diving action of whales to escape danger

species—all the animals of a certain kind (They have the same characteristics and can mate and produce young like themselves.)

Index

Bold type refers to illustrations; regular type refers to text.

Consultants

Thomas J. McIntyre, National Marine Fisheries Service/NOAA; Dr. Albert W. Erickson, University of Washington, *Chief Consultants*

Dr. Glenn O. Blough, *Educational Consultant*

Dr. Nicholas J. Long, *Consulting Psychologist*

The Special Publications and School Services Division is grateful to the individuals, organizations, and agencies named or quoted in the text and to the individuals cited here for their generous assistance: Dr. John L. Bengtson, University of Minnesota; California State Department of Fish and Game: Jack A. Ames, Robert A. Hardy, Fred E. Wendell; Kayce Cover, National Zoological Park; Dr. Kenneth C. Gordon, University of Illinois at the Medical Center; Judith M. Hobart, Beauvoir School; Ken Hollingshead, National Marine Fisheries Service/NOAA; Peter F. Major, Marine Mammal Commission; Dr. Reid Moran, San Diego Museum of Natural History; Dr. Galen B. Rathbun, U. S. Fish and Wildlife Service; Mozelle G. Richardson; Dr. William A. Richkus, Environmental Center, Martin-Marietta Corporation; Smithsonian Institution: Charles W. Potter, Dr. Clayton Ray; Dr. Jeanette Thomas, Hubbs-Sea World Research Institute.

Fred Bruemmer

Harp seal surveys its icy home in the Gulf of St. Lawrence (see cover).

Additional Reading

You may wish to check the National Geographic Index in school or public libraries for related articles. These National Geographic Society books also contain related material: *Book of Mammals*, Vol. I & II; *The Mysterious Undersea World*; *Namu*; *Wild Animals of North America*; *Wildlife Alert*; *The Blue Whale*; *The Playful Dolphins*.

The following books are also recommended:

General reading: Brown, Vinson, *Sea Mammals and Reptiles of the Pacific Coast* (New York: Macmillan, 1976). Haley, Delphine, ed., *Marine Mammals of Eastern North Pacific and Arctic Waters* (Seattle: Pacific Search Press, 1978). Martin, Richard Mark, *Mammals of the Oceans* (New York: G. P. Putnam's Sons, 1977). McClung, Robert M., *Hunted Mammals of the Sea* (New York: William Morrow & Company, 1978). Scheffer, Victor, *A Natural History of Marine Mammals* (New York: Chas. Scribner's Sons, 1976). Time-Life Television Book, *Whales and Other Sea Mammals* (New York: Time-Life Films, 1977). Waters, John F., *Some Mammals Live in the Sea* (Dodd, Mead & Company, 1972). Wise, Terence, *Whales and Dolphins* (Milwaukee: Raintree Children's Books, 1980).

Books on specific animals: Bailey, Jane H., *Sea Otter* (California: El Moro Publications, 1979). Brown, Joseph E., *Wonders of Seals and Sea Lions* (New York: Dodd, Mead & Company, 1976). Hoke, Helen, and Valerie Pitt, *Whales* (New York: Franklin Watts, Inc., 1973). Johnson, William Weber, *The Story of Sea Otters* (New York: Random House, 1973). McDearmon, Kay, *The Walrus: Giant of the Arctic Ice* (New York: Dodd, Mead & Company, 1974). Miller, Tom, *The World of the California Gray Whale* (Santa Ana, California: Baja Trail Publications, 1975). Rabinowich, Ellen, *Seals, Sea Lions, and Walruses* (New York: Franklin Watts, Inc., 1980). Scheffer, Victor, *The Year of The Seal* (New York: Chas. Scribner's Sons, 1970). Scheffer, Victor, *The Year of The Whale* (New York: Chas. Scribner's Sons, 1969). Slijper, E. J., *Whales*, 2nd ed., (New York: Cornell University Press, 1979).

Composition for *Amazing Animals of the Sea* by National Geographic's Photographic Services, Carl M. Shrader, Chief; Lawrence F. Ludwig, Assistant Chief. Printed and bound by Holladay-Tyler Printing Corp., Rockville, Md. Color separations by the Lanman-Progressive Corp., Washington, D. C.; Lincoln Graphics, Inc., Cherry Hill, N.J. *Far-out Fun!* printed by Federated Lithographers and Printers, Inc., Providence, R.I.

Library of Congress CIP Data
Main entry under title:

Amazing animals of the sea.

(Books for world explorers)
Bibliography: p.
Includes index.
SUMMARY: Discusses the characteristics and habits of the whale, dolphin, manatee, sea otter, sea lion, seal, and other marine mammals. Includes puzzles, games, and related activities.
1. Marine mammals—Juvenile literature. [1. Marine mammals. 2. Mammals] I. National Geographic Society (U. S.) II. Series.
QL713.2.A47   599.5   80-8796
ISBN 0-87044-382-8 (regular binding)   AACR2
ISBN 0-87044-387-9 (library binding)

Amazing Animals of the Sea

PUBLISHED BY
THE NATIONAL GEOGRAPHIC SOCIETY
WASHINGTON, D. C.

Gilbert M. Grosvenor, *President*
Melvin M. Payne, *Chairman of the Board*
Owen R. Anderson, *Executive Vice President*
Robert L. Breeden, *Vice President,
Publications and Educational Media*

PREPARED BY THE SPECIAL PUBLICATIONS
AND SCHOOL SERVICES DIVISION

Donald J. Crump, *Director*
Philip B. Silcott, *Associate Director*
William L. Allen, William R. Gray, *Assistant Directors*

BOOKS FOR WORLD EXPLORERS
Ralph Gray, *Editor*
Pat Robbins, *Managing Editor*
Ursula Perrin Vosseler, *Art Director*

STAFF FOR THIS BOOK
Ralph Gray, *Managing Editor*
Catherine O'Neill, Judith E. Rinard, *Writers*
Charles E. Herron, Veronica Smith, *Picture Editors*
Viviane Y. Silverman, *Designer*
Donna B. Kerfoot, Suzanne Nave Patrick, *Researchers*
Jacqueline Geschickter, *Picture Legends (Chapter 6)*
Joan Hurst, *Editorial Assistant*
Artemis S. Lampathakis, *Illustrations Secretary*

STAFF FOR FAR-OUT FUN!
Patricia N. Holland, *Project Editor;* Margaret McKelway, *Text Editor;* Loel Barr (pages 2-5, 8-15); Susanah B. Brown (page 3, bottom); Viviane Y. Silverman (pages 6-7), *Artists;* Art Iddings (pages 1, 16), *Mechanicals*

ENGRAVING, PRINTING, AND PRODUCT MANUFACTURE
Robert W. Messer, *Manager;* George V. White, *Production Manager;* Mark R. Dunlevy, *Production Project Manager;* Richard A. McClure, Raja D. Murshed, Christine A. Roberts, David V. Showers, Gregory Storer, *Assistant Production Managers;* Mary Bennett, Katherine H. Donohue, *Production Staff Assistants*

STAFF ASSISTANTS: Debra A. Antonini, Nancy F. Berry, Pamela A. Black, Nettie Burke, Jane H. Buxton, Mary Elizabeth Davis, Claire M. Doig, Rosamund Garner, Victoria D. Garrett, Nancy J. Harvey, Virginia A. McCoy, Merrick P. Murdock, Cleo Petroff, Victoria I. Piscopo, Tammy Presley, Jane F. Ray, Carol A. Rocheleau, Katheryn M. Slocum, Jenny Takacs. *Interns:* Meredith T. Jordan, Catherine S. Silcott

MARKET RESEARCH: Joe Fowler, Carrla L. Holmes, Meg McElligott, Stephen F. Moss, Marjorie E. Smith, Susan D. Snell

INDEX: Michael G. Young